Welcome to the second in a series of booklets on contemporary glass beadmakers and their craft. These book-lets will introduce you to a number of the best and most interesting contemporary glass beadmakers in the coun-try. You will get to learn more about them and their work. They will take this chance to share with us some of their favorite tools as well as some of their beadmaking secrets.

These booklets serve as companion documents to my text on glass beadmaking, **More Than You Ever Wanted To Know About Glass Beadmaking**. That text provides all the basic knowledge on glass beadmaking skills, while these booklets will show you how different artists put these skills into practice. In these adventures into beadmaking, I will assume that you have at least a passing knowledge of glass beadmaking skills, and I will not try to go into all the basics of the craft. Instead, we will focus on how these beadmakers work their wonders.

For this booklet, I have chosen to give you a glimpse into the work of another of my favorite beadmaking artists, Leah Fairbanks. She and I took our first beadmaking class together quite a while ago.

Artist Bio

Leah Fairbanks lives in Willets, California with her new husband, Derek Lusk, a lapidary artist, and their two pets, her cat and his dog. For inspiration she use to wander in the quarter-acre Zen garden designed by her landscaper father, Ben Zlataroff. It is filled with many of the same flowers that she depicts on her beads.

She grew up surrounded by art, especially by Japanese folk art. Her father often took her to tea ceremonies at the nearby Zen center where she saw many Japanese works of art. She fell in love with their bold traditional col-ors as well as the textures of the art and the paper. Her work as well as her life style continues to be influenced by oriental culture to this day.

Photo by George Post

Always expecting to earn her living as an artist, Leah studied fine art at the College of Marin and attended the San Francisco Academy of Art in 1980. She had originally intended to become a printmaker but she developed allergies to the inks.

Reluctantly she turned from printmaking to the study of glass, again at the College of Marin. She soon found herself fascinated with the brilliant colors of glass and its interplay with light. As part of this curriculum, Leah toured France visiting many of its stained glass masterpieces. At the Daum glass factory in Nancy, France, she was intrigued by the pate de verre and blown glasswork done at the factory. At the same time, she was also a little overwhelmed by the complexity of some of the glassworking techniques such as Galle-like work - overlay-ing multiple layers of different colors and then acid etching some of the glass away to form the image. Overall, she came away inspired by the experience, especially by the factory's use of themes from nature.

Shortly after returning to California, Leah's natural tendency to explore the limits of any art form led her to study neon lighting techniques. She incorporated neon into her stained glass windows and fused glass sculptures, providing them with light where none was otherwise present. Many of these neon-embellished pieces still bright-en local area homes. Neon also gave Leah her first experience in working on a torch, although neon tube bend-ing torches are a lot different from those that she now uses in making lampworked beads. Neon torches use acetylene and have jets of flame coming in from both sides of the glass to evenly heat the tubing so that it can be bent into flowing organic shapes.

Ever the experimentalist, Leah also began to incorporate other materials and "found objects" into her glasswork. Searching for her desired niche, she studied beveling at Philchuck Glass School and fusing at Camp Colton. She liked the variations in color that she could achieve by beveling or sandblasting "flashed glass," clear glass thinly coated with a transparent colored layer of glass. This process reminded her of the work to which she had been introduced at Nancy.

Then Leah discovered that a beadmaking class by Brian Kerkvliet was being offered at Fenton Glass Studio in Oakland. The lampworking flame and the fluid manipulation of the glass around a mandrel to make a bead held a special allure for her. She was hooked, attracted like a moth to the flame. Now she, and not the kiln, would decide how the glass would fuse together.

After this introduction into beadmaking, Leah went into business with another budding bead artist/friend, Kim Osibin. They shared a studio for a couple of years, feeding off of each other's creativity, and although they no longer share a studio, you can often find them on the road together teaching workshops. Leah loves teaching and working with students to develop their own style.

As before, Leah continues to do a lot of experimentation in her beadmaking, playing with different types of glass: Moretti/Effetre from Italy, Bullseye Glass from the United States, Lauscha from Germany, and Satake from Japan. She learned to control the many settings of her torch flame to manipulate each of these types of glass and for many other different operations. She works with frit, enamel and luster powders; metal foils and leaf; and a multitude of hand-pulled stringers, canes, and latticino. She incorporates all of these materials into her fanciful floral beads.

Leah was also involved in the early development of the American art glass beadmaking movement in the 1990's. She was there when a small group of beadmaking artists got together during a bead show at the Bead Museum in Prescott Arizona (now in Glendale Arizona) and formed the Society of Glass Beadmakers to promote the art of glass beadmaking. Her work on its first board of directors and in coordinating its first preplanned "Gathering" helped establish that organization on firm footing and she became deeply involved in the beadmaking scene. Her exploration of floral motifs has greatly influenced the floral beads of others.

With a lot of determination and creativity, Leah has developed into one of this country's leading beadmakers. When at home, she works in bursts at the torch, often hours at a time. With her torch blazing and her creative juices flowing, she frequently loses track of time until she is so famished she just has to stop. On her off days, she works on cleaning, stringing and pricing her work as well as developing new designs.

Leah works almost exclusively in floral beads, inspired by the exotic irises and orchids that grow in her Northern California garden. Recurrent motifs in her work include wheat, irises, berries, lavender, bonsai, Earth Goddesses, Angels and Mermaids. Her Tapestry series of autumn leaves high-lights her use of mixed metals, while her Monet series paints intricate land-scapes in a variety of floral scenes. Leah's finished jewelry interweaves her hand-made beads with multiple strands of unique semi-precious stones and fresh water pearls, evolving into one-of-a-kind treasures. She incorporates numerous techniques to brighten and detail her beads, some of which she will share in this booklet. She has also begun collaborating with metal workers and her husband, a lapidary artist, to develop new facets to her art. Let's look at some of her work.

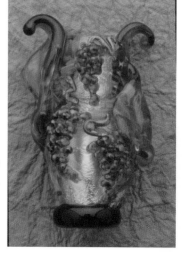

Vessel-shaped bead with drapery handles and adorned with bunches of grapes. The body of the vessel is made using gold leaf cased in light transparent amber.

Photo by: George Post

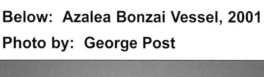
Below: Azalea Bonzai Vessel, 2001
Photo by: George Post

Above: Golden Iris Necklace, 1998
Photo by: George Post

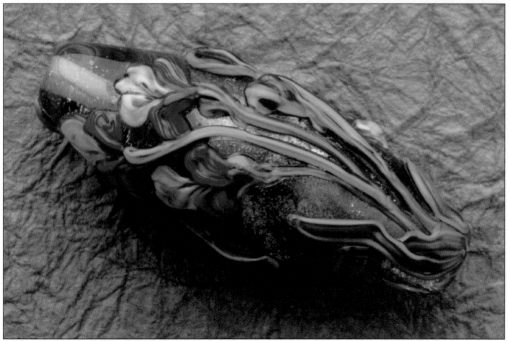

Left:
Iris Bead, 1998
Photo by:
George Post

Below: Iris Moon Necklace, 2001

Left: Detail of Back

Metal Work by: Deborah Nishihara

Photo by: George Post

Below: Two Grape Medallions, 2000

Left: Red Flame   Right: Merlot

Photo by: George Post

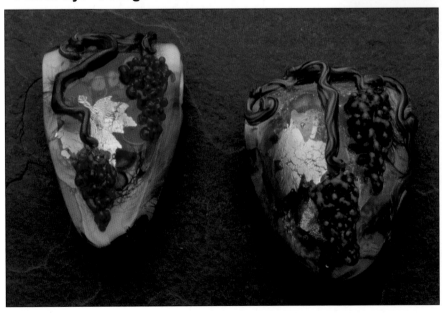

Above: Japanese Plum Blossom, 2001

Photo by: George Post

Above: Japanese Plum Blossom, 2000

Photo by: George Post

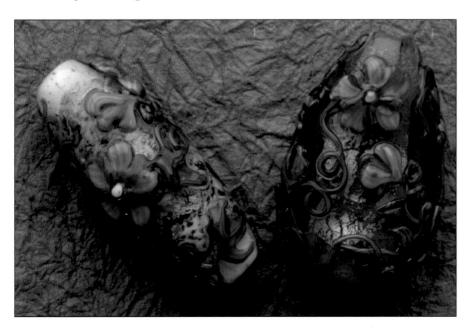

Left:

Two Morning Glory

Beads, 1998

Photo by:

George Post

Left:

Multi-colored Iris Medallion, 2000

Photo by: George Post

Below: Assorted Floral Beads, 1998
Photo by: George Post

Above: Fuchsias on Red Brick Urn, 1999
Photo by: George Post

Below: Plum Blossom Urn, 2000
Photo by: George Post

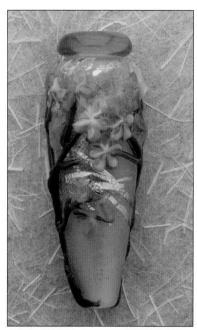

Above: Gladiola Oval, 2001
Photo by: George Post

Above: Gladiola Urn, 2001
Photo by: George Post

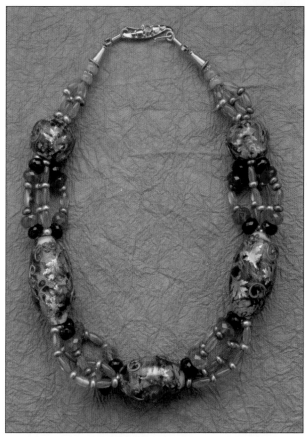

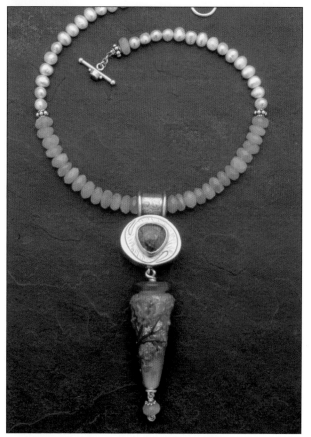

Above: Tapestry Necklace, 1998
Photo by: George Post

Above: Moulin Rouge, 2001
Metal Work by: Deborah Nishihara
Photo by: George Post

Cased Cane

Leah uses a lot of cased glass canes in her work to help provide some natural looking variation of color in constructing the flowers and vegetation on her beads. As a general rule, she uses dark transparent colors to case light opaque colors. The light opaque color on the inside of the cane reflects back more of the light coming through the transparent color, making the transparent color more visible. The darkness of the transparent color increases the richness of color and its visibility even when drawn out into a fine cane.

Leah makes her cased canes by winding the glass from a dark transparent colored rod onto a light opaque colored rod as if she were winding glass onto a mandrel. This is what she is doing in the first two photos to the left. The trick to casing this way is to apply the transparent glass fairly hot while at the same time keeping the opaque colored rod cool enough that it is not flopping back and forth. This process is complicated by the fact that as they get hot, the transparent colored glasses tend to be much stiffer than opaque glasses. As you can see by the photos here, she does a good job at this.

If the opaque rod does start flopping around, chill it and push it back into place with a paddle or marver. A mini-marver mounted on your torch, as shown in the third photo, comes in handy when doing this because it is almost like having a third hand. You can hold onto the opaque rod in one hand, the transparent rod in your other hand and push the bending opaque rod section back into place with the mini-marver, all at the same time.

Keep wrapping the transparent rod around the opaque rod all the way to the end of the opaque rod, making sure that each wrap of the transparent glass lies right next to the previous one. If possible, you also want to avoid trapping air between the wraps. Leah avoids this by slightly twisting the transparent rod clockwise as she winds it onto the opaque rod. This twisting motion pushes the hottest portion of the rod right into the crease underneath the previous wrap, forcing the hot glass into any small cavities at the base of the previous wrap.

As she completes the last wrap, Leah swings the transparent rod around to the free end of the cased opaque rod as shown in the fourth photo and starts heating the cased region in preparation for pulling it out into cane. She gets the whole cased region hot and marvers out the creases between the wraps. She then heats it until the whole cased region is hot to the core and slowly pulls it out into about a one to two millimeter diameter cane, as shown in the

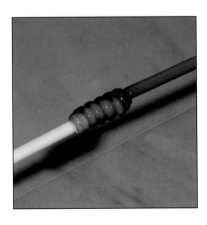
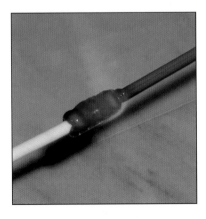
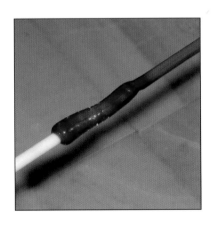

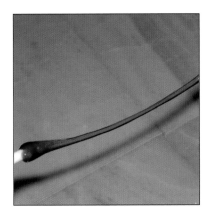  

next few photos. This size is perfect for painting flowers and leaves onto a bead, as you will soon see.

By constructing her cased canes in this manner, Leah ends up with a fairly thick casing of transparent glass relative to the finished cane, about one third of the diameter of the finished cane. She likes the rich color variation that she gets from this ratio of transparent to opaque glass. You can increase the casing thickness further by adding a second wrap layer to the casing or you can decrease the thickness by wrapping the opaque rod with cane instead of another rod. These variations would change the depth of color and the amount of light bouncing back from the opaque glass.

Doubly Cased Cane

The first variation of cased cane described above is known as doubly cased cane. Its construction is shown in the photos on this page and is very similar to that of singly cased cane. You may want to use doubly cased canes with encasements of multiple transparent colors instead of singly cased canes to get greater color variation in your floral decorations.

In the example shown here, Leah demonstrates making a doubly cased cane that she uses to make grape clusters and violets. First, she cases an opaque white rod with a thin inner layer of transparent cobalt and follows by adding a thick outer layer of transparent amethyst. The two layers give the cane more depth, and creates a color that is not present in the Effetre palette.

As you can see in the first photo of this section (top center photo), Leah starts making the doubly cased cane by wrapping the opaque white rod with a thin layer of transparent cobalt glass. She gets the thinner layer by applying the transparent cobalt glass hotter than she did for the singly cased cane on the previous page. When she has finished applying the first casing layer, she marvers it to smooth it out, making it less likely that she will trap air as she applies the second casing layer.

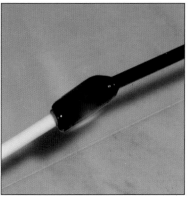

Then, as you see in the second and third photos to the right, she wraps on the second layer of transparent amethyst. This glass layer is applied cooler and thicker than the first layer, as is evident in the more rope-like nature of these wraps that you see in the next photo. To stretch out the construction into doubly cased cane, she again heats it up, marvers it out, reheats it thoroughly, and slowly draws it out into a one to two millimeter thick cane.

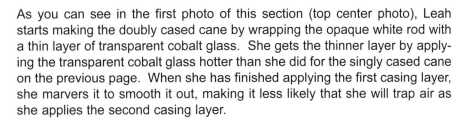

Ribbed cane

Ribbed cane is cased cane that has had some extra color variation added around the circumference of the cane. This variation makes the cased cane look more organic, and gives it a vein-like structure similar to that which you see in many leaves and flowers. I have described one form of ribbed cane construction in my text on beadmaking, but the technique that Leah presents here is different and may be easier for novices.

Leah starts out by pulling a stringer of the striating color. The striating color is usually a dark opaque, such as black or blue. It has to be rather dark to remain visible when the ribbed cane is pulled out to final size. To pull a stringer, she starts by using the heat of the flame to melt the end of a glass rod into a medium sized ball, as seen in the top photo. Then she removes the rod from the flame and pinches a small section of the gather with sharp pointed tweezers and slowly pulls a stringer out of the ball as seen in the next two photos. There are two points to remember when doing this: first, the slower that you pull the stringer from the ball the thicker it will be, and second, you have to pull harder and faster as time goes on because the glass in the ball is getting cooler and stiffer. You want to pull a stringer approximately a millimeter in diameter.

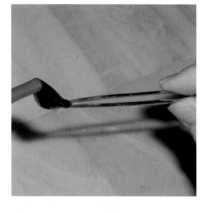

Pinching off just the right amount of glass with your tweezers to pull out the stringer can be a little tricky for a novice, but it is quick and easy to do once mastered. An alternate method would be to pull out the stringer by touching a prewarmed glass rod to the ball of glass and use it to stretch out the glass.

Once she has the dark opaque stringer in hand, Leah next constructs a cased cane as was described in the previous section, by winding a dark transparent glass onto a light opaque rod, as in the lower left photo. After all the glass is wound on, she smoothes out the casing by heating it up and marvering it out as was shown for doubly cased cane. When the casing is smooth as in the bottom center photo it is ready to receive the ribbing. The casing has to be smooth prior to adding the dark opaque stringer so that the stringer is fully supported on the casing. If this is not done, any unsupported stringer may burn through and ball up as you heat the construction.

Now it is time to apply the dark opaque stringer to the outside of the casing. This has to be done off to one side of the flame because the stringer is so small in diameter that it heats up and melts very quickly when introduced into the flame. By keeping the cane in this cooler location in the flame, it will not heat up as quickly, and will stay more manageable.

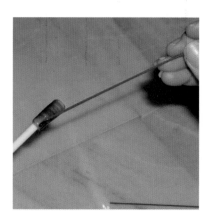

At the same time, it is important to prewarm the cased rod enough that the hot stringer will stick to it. How you coordinate these two tasks depends upon how you like to apply your stringer; left-to-right or right-to-left. If you apply it left-to-right as Leah is doing in the first picture on this page, you should be working in the left side of the flame. You preheat the cased rod in the flame and slowly slide it to the left as you apply the stringer in the left edge of the flame. As you do this, the position of the stringer in the flame essentially stays the same, and the cased rod preheat and the stringer application are both part of the same motion. If you like to apply your stringer right-to-left, you should be working in the right side of the flame using a corresponding but opposite motion.

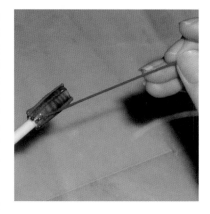

As you apply the stringer, you also want to remember to have it run over the edge of the casing on both ends as seen in the second photo on this page. This step will help ensure that you stretch out the stringer as well as the cased rod when you draw out your ribbed cane.

Now Leah is ready to draw out the construction into a usable cane for use on her floral beads. To do this, she attaches a hot rod to the end of the construction, swirling the hot glass around the end of the casing to uniformly coat and attach the rod to the end of the ribbed construction. Covering the end of the bundle ensures that you get as much usable ribbed cane as possible out of the draw. Note: if you do not completely case the end of the glass bundle, it is possible that the beginning of your cane will not have any ribbing because you are pulling the center out of the construction.

Be sure to heat the construction enough that the stringer melts into the casing before you start to draw out the cane, as seen in the lower right photo. This will assist in drawing out the construction correctly. The picture below shows a flower made using ribbed cane. Notice the natural looking striations that the ribs give to the cane.

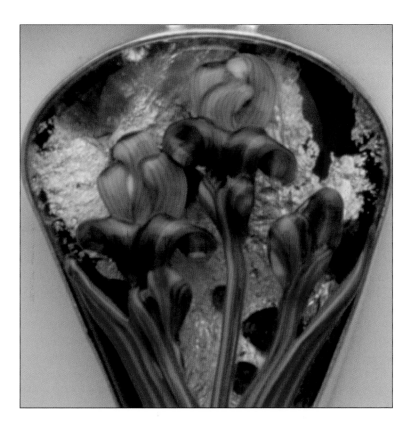

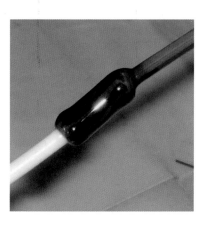

Branch Cane

Leah calls this branch cane because she uses it to make her tree branches and grape vines. It is really just partially cased cane. The difference here is that she is casing opaque glass over opaque glass and applying incomplete stripes of color. This gives the cane some variation of color, and makes the branches appear more natural.

To make this type of cane, Leah starts out by warming an opaque brown rod and melting the end of an opaque black rod. Then she adds a stripe of black about an inch long down the length of the brown rod as seen in the top photo. She does this by touching the hot black rod to the end of the warm brown one and drawing the black rod toward her, as in the second photo to the left. She is aiming the torch flame onto the black rod right at the spot where it meets the brown rod. This preheats the casing rod as she swipes it onto the rod being cased. You will notice that the black stripes should not be right next to each other. You want to be able to see brown glass between them.

After applying stripes of black down the brown rod, Leah then adds a couple more stripes using thick gray stringer to get more color variation. Striping with both rod and stringer creates stripes of different widths achieving more variation in the finished product. Notice that she applies this gray stringer left-to-right by working it in the left side of the flame, as she did in making ribbed cane.

Once Leah has all the different colored stripes applied, she heats up the whole construction. Before it is to the point where it is ready to pull out into cane, she twists up the whole construction somewhat, as seen in the bottom center photo. This twist introduces even more color variation into the cane. You can get a feeling for how much she has twisted the construction by looking at the left side of the bottom right photo where she is pulling this construction out into cane.

She uses this cane by drawing branches onto the bead, and leaves it raised on the surface. She does not usually do any extra twisting of the cane as she applies it to the bead but does add multiple layers for increased effect.

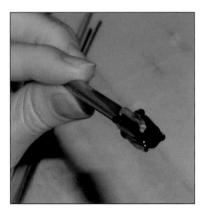

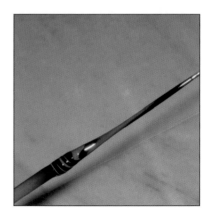

Use of Canes to Construct Floral Decorations

Now that you know how to make cased, ribbed and branch canes, you need to learn to apply them to create floral decorations. We look first at how to use cased canes.

In the simplest application of cased canes, you apply it onto the surface of the bead like a stringer to form stems and tendrils. For this kind of application, Leah generally uses opaque white cased with transparent dark emerald. As you can see in the photo to the right, the white core causes the green to appear to be a lighter shade in the center of applied decorations and darker along the edges. The other thing that you will notice is that Leah leaves these decorations raised on the surface of the bead, as she does with most of her decorations. She feels that this gives them a greater feeling of depth and gives them a pleasant tactile feel.

To look more life-like, these stems and tendrils should not be straight. Thick stems will usually have a slight curve to them as they take up the weight of the flower or the leaves while thinner vines and tendrils will weave and meander over the surface of the bead. If you are trying to depict plants growing out of the ground rather than still life clusters, then you need to establish an up and down direction on the bead and grow your stems from the ground to the sky, sticking to that orientation over the entire bead surface.

When making a tree, a single branch cane application is not sufficient to portray the mass of the trunk. Here you will have to apply multiple layers of branch cane on top of each other to build up the trunk. At its base, you will have exposed roots separating out of the trunk, just as you have branches breaking out at the top of the tree. Generally, the branches are thicker near the trunk and twigs coming off of the branches are smaller. Likewise, the trunk of the tree is generally a little thicker near its base than at the top.

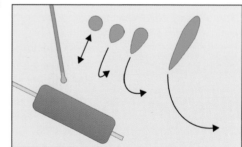

Another simple type of decoration that you can make with cased canes are leaf-like shapes, as seen in the figure to the left. Here you have a rounded structure on one end that is pulled to a point on the other end. To make this type of decoration, you heat up the end of your cased cane to form a small ball of hot glass, touch it to the bead, and pull the cane away in sort of a glancing blow.

How you do this blow affects the shape of the leaf. If you go straight in and out from the surface of the bead, you will get a dot. If you go straight in and then pull out at a slight angle, you will get a dot with a slight tail. If you come in at a slight angle and then pull away at an angle, the base of the leaf will be less pronounced and the leaf will get longer. This can be varied somewhat to give your leaves all sorts of dimensions. You can also apply the stringer for a short distance along the bead to fabricate long leaves such as you have on agapanthus.

The other thing that you can do when applying leaves to the surface of a bead is to change the plane of the stroke as you apply the leaf. When the motion of the cane is all in one plane, you get leaves as we see in the second photo on the left. However, if you swing the cane out of that plane as you pull away you will get leaves that curl to one side or the other depending on which way you swing, as seen to the left.

For bigger leaves, like on violets, you can apply two of the same leaf strokes that we just discussed side by side. The trick here is pulling the point of the leaves to the same point as seen to the right. Of course leaves do not just hang in space. They are connected to the rest of the plant by branches, stems, and tendrils. For flowers and other types of green vegetation, you will use the green cased cane to connect the rounded section of the leaf as in figure below and to the left. For trees and other deciduous bushes you will use branch cane to connect to the leaves. Long spiky vegetation like agapanthus will usually extend up from the ground as depicted in the right side of the figure.

After you have mastered leaves, you can then move on to making flowers. One of the simplest kinds of flowers to construct is a rose. They are made by simply spiraling cased cane onto the surface of a bead, as seen to the right. Some artists purposely make their spirals sloppier than this, overlapping the cane as they go. They believe that the increased color variation produced this way makes a rose that looks more realistic.

Roses come in an abundance of colors, so you can use all sorts of cased canes to make them. Some examples that Leah uses include the following transparent colors cased over opaque white: ruby pink, yellow, purple, orange, amethyst, etc. Let your imagination go wild. Leah will demonstrate a rose bead later in this booklet.

The other kinds of flowers that Leah makes have more defined petals, which she makes using the same basic stroke that she uses for leaves. It is how they are clustered that defines what kind of flowers they are. There are fundamentally two different variations in the constructing the petals around the center of the flower; the strokes can go toward the center of the flower or they can radiate outward from it . Orchids have them pointing toward the center of the flower while wild flowers have them pointing away from the center. This difference is illustrated to the left.

Another petal variation that you see in nature is how pointed or rounded the ends of the flower petals are. Some flowers like gladiolus are quite pointed while others like daisies are more rounded. These differences are illustrated to the right. Leah will demonstrate making a daisy bead later in this booklet.

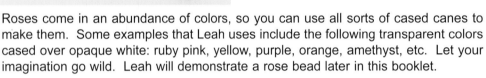

These were relatively simple arrangements of petals because the strokes were either all pointed toward the center of the flower or all were pointed away. Other flowers may

not have all the petals pointed in the same direction. As an example, Leah makes her orchids with five strokes. Each flower has three strokes down to the center and two strokes down away from the center, one on each side, as seen in the figure to the left. The other thing that we see about these strokes is that sometimes you need to be specific about where the stroke is pointed. Here both of the bottom strokes are pointed down and not radially away from the center. The stem will come in at the bottom between these two strokes.

Another thing to notice about the previous example is that the strokes do not take up the entire area around the center. The bottom and the sides of the flower are more open. You can see something similar in Leah's sweet peas, which have four strokes to the center all in the top half of the flower, as seen to the right.

Similarly, Leah makes her violets with five center-pointing strokes. They are of varying width and do not completely fill in the space around the center. They are similar to the orchid, with three thinner strokes down at the top and but with two inward strokes at the bottom (where the orchid strokes were outward). The stems on these flowers may come in at any of the three gaps in the distribution of petals; the left, the bottom, or the right.

The other thing that you can do to add a more life-like look when making your floral decorations is to use ribbed cane rather than cased cane. This adds a lot of extra color variation to the flowers, which makes them look much more natural, and gives a feeling of multiple petals with a single stroke. As an example of this, look back at the sweet peas above. Notice how alive the ribbed cane makes it look.

Well, enough of theory for the moment. Let's watch Leah make a few floral beads to see how it is done.

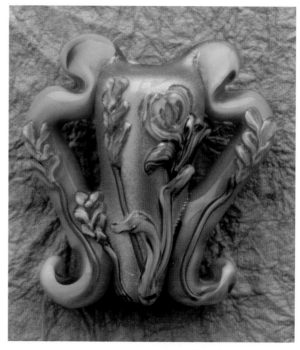

Floral Urn   **Photo by George Post**

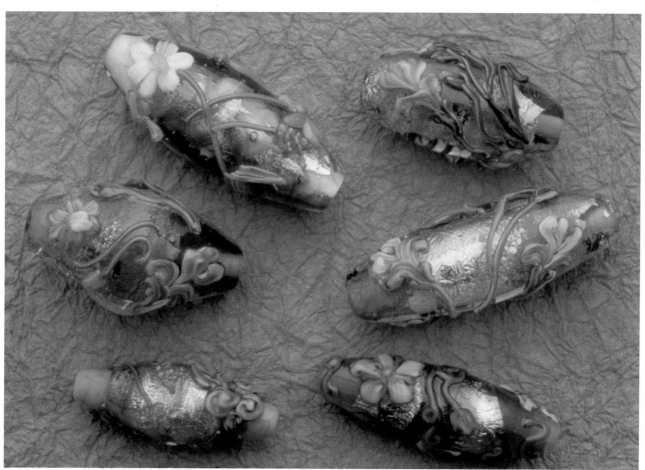

Collection of Floral Beads   **Photo by: George Post**

Rose Bead

The first bead that Leah will demonstrate for us is a rose bead. In this bead, multiple roses of several colors are clustered together as if in a corsage, with decorative foliage filling out the rest of the bead. This bead uses only cased canes.

As seen in the photos in this section, Leah first constructs a large torpedo bead on which to place her floral decorations. She starts by winding a first layer of glass the whole length of the bead. She works with the glass relatively cool, reheating and marvering as necessary to get the desired shape. She marvers at multiple stages as she builds up of the bead, checking its shape as she goes.

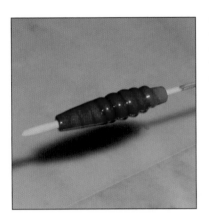

After she has established the length of the bead, Leah goes back and adds extra glass to the bead to build up its thickness in desired areas. The second photo shows the bead in transition. She has added extra glass mainly to the center of the bead and has started marvering out the left side into its final torpedo shape. This photo allows you to see where she has added the glass and how it spreads out and flows as it is marvered.

In the third photo, Leah is just completing the final shaping of the bead using her paddle. She has a long torpedo with a smooth oval center. If Leah is decorating the background of a bead, she adds it first and carefully shapes the bead before starting to add any surface floral decorations. This is because she likes to have her floral decorations raised so that they have more depth to them. Working the final shape of the bead after adding the floral decorations would require melting them into the surface of the bead and loss of the raised aspect of her work.

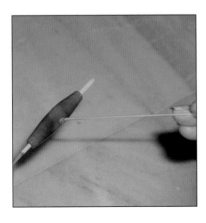

Leah now starts to add the roses to the bead. She has chosen to add two clusters of roses more or less directly opposite each other around the circumference of the bead. You could add more clusters or position them so that they are less symmetric to vary your layout. In this case, though, she will be varying the size and distribution of roses within each cluster to add a little extra dimension to the piece.

To make her roses, Leah just applies a spiral of cased cane to the surface of the bead, winding from the center of the flower outward. She is not overlapping the cane, but could, if she wanted more color variation or greater visual depth in the flower. For the first few roses she is using a cane of white

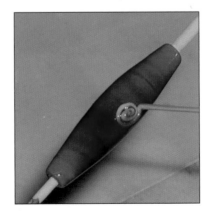

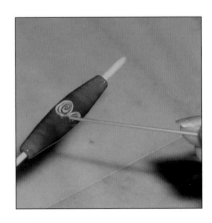

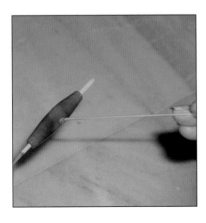

16

© 2001, James Kervin

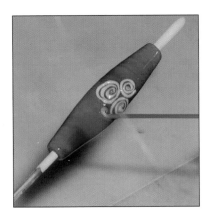

cased with ruby pink and for the others she is using white cased with dark lavender. To keep the cased cane from frying, she is working off to the right side of the flame where it is cooler. She is keeping the base bead just hot enough to accept the cane.

She adds the second rose right next to the first one, as seen in the last photo on the previous page. To do this, she has to have a feeling for how big the second rose is going to be so that she knows where to begin before starting to spiral the cane onto the bead.

As you can see by the first photo on this page, she has chosen to have three pink roses in this cluster and finishes all three before starting to add any of the lavender roses. In the next photo, you can see that she has chosen to make the lavender roses smaller than the pink roses and to place them at the outside edge of the cluster.

In the second photo, you can see the final balance in the placement of both sets of roses on this side of the bead. Leah has clustered the pink roses into a triangular arrangement with the purple roses in another triangular arrangement but pointing in the opposite direction. On the backside of the bead, as seen in the last photo on this page, she has chosen to use perpendicular clusters of two roses of each color. This arrangement has sort of a figure eight look to it. Notice how well the two colors of roses nestle together in this arrangement.

After Leah has the rose clusters completed, she starts to add rose leaves coming out of the clusters using cased cane of transparent emerald over opaque white. As you can see, she tends to have these coming out of the joints between two roses. In the two upper right photos, you can see how she makes the leaves by touching down at the base of the leaf and then pulling it to a point.

The last two photos on this page show the two sides of the finished rose bead with the two different cluster configurations. You can also see how she has filled up much of the remaining blank area on the bead with leaves and tendrils of green vegetation. She curls these on for effect by working in the side of the torch flame in much the same way she did in applying the roses to the surface of the bead.

Daisy Bead

The bead that Leah will demonstrate in this section also has a collection of flowers distributed over its surface. The flowers in this bead are daisies of different colors with leaves added to fill out some of the remaining blank areas on the bead. The daisies are constructed from outward strokes of ribbed cane as was discussed earlier.

Leah starts out by constructing a round bead about three-quarters of an inch long. She builds it up pretty much the same way she did in making the long torpedo bead of the last example. She winds the bead to length and then adds extra layers of glass to rough out the shape of the bead, as shown in the upper left photo. She then rounds out the bead by heating it up in the flame and allowing surface tension to suck in the glass. This application of heat also smoothes out the surface of the bead. Like the last bead, she does not add any extra background decoration to the bead before applying her floral decorations.

To begin the daisies with which she will decorate this bead, Leah applies a yellow dot at four places equally spaced around the equator of the bead, as seen in the third photo to the left. The dots serve as the central section of each daisy and establish their location on the bead. They are applied by dotting an opaque yellow rod through the flame onto the bead. The dots are kept raised, as are all of Leah's decorations.

In the rest of the photos at the bottom of this page, we see Leah applying petals onto the daisies. In the first photo, we see that she has applied two lavender petals to the first daisy. The ribbed cane that she is using for the first two daisies is transparent lavender over opaque white with black ribbing. To apply a petal, she melts a small ball onto the end of the cane, touches it to the bead, pushing it right against the edge of the yellow dot. Then she strokes the ribbed cane radially away from the center of the dot to form the petals before pulling up and burning away at its end, as she is doing in this photo.

When she burns off the end of the stretched petals, she pulls them to a point. These petals are not as pointed as some of her other flowers because she has burned them off close to the surface of the bead. She adds six of these petals spaced equally around the dot. She first makes one flower of this ribbed cane and then a second of the same cane at the dot on the opposite side of the bead.

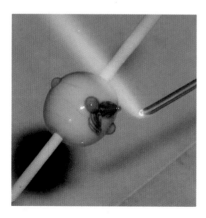
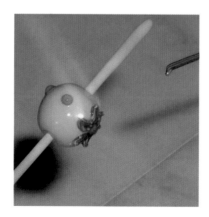

At this point, Leah switches to a ribbed cane of a second color. This one is made from transparent cobalt over an opaque white core with black ribbing. She uses this cane to construct the other two daisies on this bead at the remaining two yellow dots. The petals for these two daisies are made the same way as the first two, by stroking from the center dot radially outward and burning them off close to the surface of the bead.

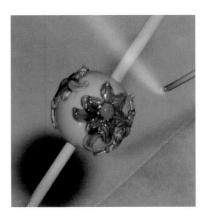

Once she has completed all four of the daisies, Leah adds leaves of her transparent emerald over opaque white cased cane to embellish them. These leaves are applied as long sweeping strokes, emerging from the gaps between flower petals and curving out onto the surface of the bead as seen in the photos above.

In the second photo, Leah has just added the leaf in the upper left of the bead. Here you can see how much of a curl that she adds to some of her leaves. The leaf at the bottom of the photo has about a 45-degree curl to it. Curling the leaves like this allows them to occupy and enrich more of the bead surface. This makes the bead more interesting.

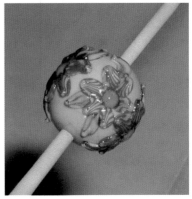

In the next photo and the rest of those on this page, you can see how Leah distributes the curls of her leaves. They do not all curl in the same direction. In this photo, she has the newly added leaf in the center curling to the right and both of the ones below it curling to the left. In the bottom two photos, you can also see some leaves that are not curled but just come out straight from between the petals.

On this bead, Leah adds three curled leaves to each of the flowers; two at the top and one at the bottom of each of the two blue daisies. This pattern is reversed on the purple daisies. Distributing the leaves like this provides better coverage of the bead and ensures balance between the daisies. Leah curls each leaf to whichever direction helps to fill more of the bead surface.

Finally the bead is done. We see a close up of a blue and a purple daisy in the last two photographs on this page. The bead is then popped into the annealer to relieve any residual stresses.

With these last two beads you get a feeling for the simplicity of how a few strokes of glass cane can make a beautiful floral decoration. From this point on, Leah embellishes more on this theme while also adding interesting backgrounds to the beads.

Using Foils and Leaf

Leah likes to decorate the backgrounds of her beads to provide additional interesting detail to attract the eye. She often cases these backgrounds with clear glass to give a greater feeling of depth to the bead. One of the techniques that she uses to decorate her backgrounds is to apply metal foils or leaf to them.

Leah uses gold, silver, and palladium in her work. The metals come in booklets like the gold and silver leaf booklets seen in the upper left photo. Each of the pieces of very thin metal is supported on a tissue page in the booklet. The pages keep the metal separated and flat. They also protect them from ripping, as they are quite fragile.

Foil and leaf differ only in thickness. Foil is about thirty times thicker than leaf, on the order of 0.0003" thick, and is primarily available in silver. This is one third of the thickness of kitchen aluminum foil. At this thickness the metal is quite easy to handle. You can pick it up, as Leah is doing in the second photo in this series, and it won't tear or crumble up into almost nothing, as silver leaf would.

For this example, Leah only wants to cover the center section of the bead. To accomplish this task, she cuts a strip of foil about an inch wide off of her sheet, using scissors. She cuts the strip long enough so that it will wrap around the circumference of the bead about one and a quarter times. She usually lays the foil strip onto a paddle, from which she will pick it up with a hot bead. In this case, she is going to pick it up from a marble work surface.

Next she finishes up the shape of the bead. Here she has constructed a long torpedo bead to the center of which she is going to add the foil. She then reheats the bead and picks up the foil by rolling the bead onto it. Once she has the foil rolled up around the bead, Leah then burnishes it onto the bead surface to make sure that it is firmly attached. In this case, she burnishes it by rolling the bead on her paddle. Foil and leaf have to be firmly attached to the surface of the bead to prevent them from melting off when they are subsequently exposed to the torch flame.

Leaf is much thinner than foil, on the order of 0.0000035" thick for gold leaf and 0.00001" thick for silver. This will vary some between manufacturers. Because it is so thin, leaf has very little strength and is hard to handle. In the first picture on the next page, Leah is tearing some palladium leaf off of a sheet in her book. Notice how fragile it is as she rips a little bit at a time using her mandrel. It is almost impossible to try and pick this up and cut it with

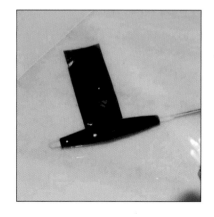

scissors. In the next photo, Leah lays out some leaf onto her work surface. Notice how it wrinkles up. It is very difficult to get leaf to lie flat.

About the only way to handle leaf with any success is to keep it trapped between sheets of tissue or paper. If you want to cut it with scissors, you have to cut the leaf and the tissue at the same time and then slowly peel off the top sheet of tissue before turning the rest of the stack over onto your marver. Some people are successful in using a small paintbrush to move the leaf around on their marvers, but even this can be tricky.

It is best to keep this remaining sheet of tissue in place on the leaf until you are ready to use it. You may want to weigh down the tissue so that it does not blow around on you. Then, just before you are ready to use the leaf, carefully remove the tissue so as not to disturb the leaf. You can then pick it up off of the marver by rolling a hot bead across it.

Another option is to try to pick up the leaf with tweezers and apply it as Leah is shown doing in the series of photos on this page. She chooses to use this technique for one of two reasons: either she wants to add a rough irregularly shaped piece of leaf to the bead, or the bead is not circular in cross section and thus is not easily rolled over the leaf. In the upper right photo, Leah is applying palladium leaf onto a torpedo bead using tweezers. Here she is applying it as a rough shape with frayed edges.

The last three photos show Leah using whole sheets of gold leaf to cover the surface of one of her urn beads. She picks up the sheet of leaf and applies it to the bead, trying to smooth it over as much of the surface as possible. When you do this, you will be amazed at how fast the leaf gets sucked up onto the bead. Unless you take great care to try to spread it over the surface, you will only get a small section of the bead covered with the leaf. Here you can see that with the first sheet she got only the first half of the bead covered. She is able to cover the other side with the second sheet.

In the last photo, Leah is burnishing the gold leaf onto the bead surface by rubbing over it with her tweezers. This pushes it firmly against the surface so that it does not immediately burn off when hit with the torch. Even when well burnished, it is still possible to burn leaf off if you heat it too much. If you do, gold leaf may leave a muddy look on the bead and silver may leave a brown deposit.

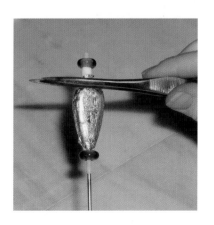

If you want your leaf to be more resistant to the flame, you need to case it with clear glass. If you case just part of the leaf, you can burn off the rest. to get patterned foiled areas on a bead.

Sweet Pea Bead

The next bead that Leah will demonstrate is decorated with random sweet pea blossoms on a variegated colored background of glass frit applied over palladium foil. She prefers to use this type of background for her floral beads, rather than the monotone backgrounds used in the previous examples. If she wants the floral blossoms to stand out more clearly from the background, she will often encase it in a layer of clear glass before applying the floral decorations.

Leah starts out by forming another of her long slender torpedo beads. In the second photo, she applies a rough partial coating of palladium leaf using some of the techniques discussed in the previous section. She tears a ragged piece out of the book and applies it randomly with her tweezers, being sure to keep plenty of open space on the bead. She then burnishes the leaf onto the surface. Palladium is an easy metal to work with because it is more resistant to heat. Once burnished into place, it does not burn off of the bead as gold and silver sometimes do. It stays very bright, reflecting most of the light striking it. This reflection enhances any transparent glass that is applied over the palladium.

Next Leah lays out some frit (granules of glass) onto her graphite pad. She makes this frit herself from the end of constructions that do not get completely pulled out into cane. These include cased, ribbed or any other type of cane that she makes for use in her work. She just snips the hot glass off with her tile cutters into a can of water that she keeps on her workbench. The sudden shock of the cold water causes the glass to break up into small pieces. There are just a few kinds of glass that she does not save for this purpose. She does not save opalino or alabastro colors or any of the filigrana with the white centers. These are not completely compatible with other glasses in the Effetre palette.

Leah likes frit about the size of sesame seeds or smaller. If the frit is not small enough for her, she may try to thermal shock them a second time. She does this by laying the pieces out onto a small kiln shelf, which she puts into her annealer. She heats the annealer up to about 950°F. After turning off the annealer, she goes into it using heavily insulated gloves that can be purchased from a fusing supplier. She pulls the kiln shelf out of the annealer and pours the hot glass into a metal container of water before returning the shelf to the annealer. Metal containers are preferred because the hot glass may melt through the bottom of a plastic container. A turkey-roasting pan is ideal for this purpose because it is cheap and long. This means that you do

not have to jockey the extremely hot kiln shelf around trying to pour all of the hot glass into the water.

Often the glass will still be too coarse, so Leah will throw some into a coffee grinder, which is used only for this purpose, and grind it for a few seconds. Avoid breathing any of the fine dust during this process because it is potentially toxic and can scar your lungs similar to asbestos. Some people do not like to use fine powder and screen it out. Large chunks are also not usually desired so pick them out. Since the glass chews up the grinder blade, Leah will pass a magnet over the frit to pull any filings out of it.

If you do not have all of this frit paraphernalia, you can always make some by wrapping your glass ends in newspaper and beating on them with a hammer. Be sure to wear protective goggles when you do this.

With the frit laid out on her marver, Leah heats up the bead to the point where the outside surface just starts to glow and get soft. The she rolls the bead across the pile of frit as seen in the third photo on the previous page. If the bead is not hot enough, it will not pick up any frit. Then she returns it to the flame to get it hot enough to pick up more frit. After a couple of cycles, she builds up a good layer of frit on the bead, as seen in the lower left photo on the previous page. How much frit you add is an individual artistic choice. Leah then heats up the bead and marvers the frit flat into the surface as seen in the bottom center photo on the previous page.

To introduce more variety to the background, Leah adds a strip of dichroic glass to the bead. Dichroic glass has a coating on one side of the glass that lets some colors of light go through, but not others. (This is a vast simplification and if you want more information on the subject refer to my bead-making text.) When applying dichroic glass, you heat it on the uncoated side while pushing the coated side down against the bead surface. This is what she is doing in the last photo on the previous page. As you can see by the first photo on this page, she is not trying to completely cover the entire surface of the bead with dichroic glass. Instead, she is just partially covering the bead with a spiral of dichroic.

The reason that you heat the uncoated side of dichroic glass is that the coating can burn off in the flame. So the next thing that Leah does is to get the dichroic coating pushed up against the bead surface, just as she had to burnish the leaf to prevent it from burning off. Leah uses two techniques to attach the dichroic to the bead. The first is to grab the edges of the strip with

her tweezers and stretch the clear glass backing over the surface of the bead, as seen in the top center photo. The second technique is to heat up the dichroic strip and marver the clear glass backing so that it spreads out and completely covers the coating.

Once you have the dichroic coating firmly attached to the surface of the bead and completely encased by the clear backing, the bead can be worked at a higher temperature to finish shaping it without fear of burning the dichroic coating. Eventually, Leah gets the bead back into a nice torpedo shape with all of the background complete, as in the fourth picture on the previous page.

Now it is time to start applying the floral decorations onto the background. For this bead, Leah chooses to apply the sweet peas with all the blossoms pointed in one direction around the circumference of the bead, rather than orientating the design on the bead with one end up and one end down. This circumferential direction will be orientated up in all of the photos that you will see here.

Leah makes her sweet pea blossoms using four downward strokes of ribbed cane toward the center of the flower, as she is doing in the last two photos on the previous page. Petals do not go all the way around the center of the flower, they are only put on the upper half of the flower. In these photos, we can see how she is distributing the blossoms over the surface of the bead.

After all of the sweet pea blossoms have been added, Leah adds the flower stems and tendrils. This is what she is applying in the first two photos on this page. Each of the sweet pea blossoms has a stem or tendril that comes out of the bottom of the blossom and swirls about the surface of the bead. These decorations are made from cased canes of transparent emerald over opaque white. She applies them as free flowing loops on the surface of the bead, filling in much of the area between the blossoms. You can see in the photos that Leah is working in the right side of the flame as she swirls on the tendrils.

In the third photo, Leah is adding an additional sweet pea blossom to a location that she felt was a little bare. With that done, the bead is finished. We

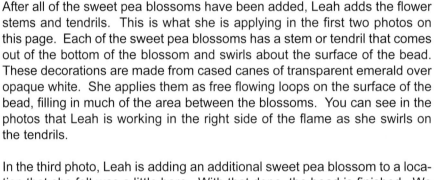

can see two different views of the finished bead at the bottom of this page. See how much more alive the textured background makes this bead look. This is why Leah likes to use complex backgrounds on her floral beads.

Monet Bead

Leah calls this design, her Monet bead, because the light pastel colors on the silver foil background give it the feel of a Monet painting. The floral decorations that she applies over this background are violets. With these floral decorations, she creates an up end and a down end on the bead to which she orients the flowers.

Leah starts with another nice slender torpedo bead and adds a complete wrap of silver foil around the central section of the bead, as was discussed earlier. Many times when adding foil like this, it may not firmly attach to the bead, and can peel off later if not anchored down. Anchoring requires adding a partial or complete glass casing onto the foil, expecially the edges, to hold it in place. If nothing else, it is important to cover the exposed edges of the foil. In this bead, this is not a problem because Leah is going to add a random decorative background of transparent glass over the entire surface of the silver.

To create the random coating of transparent glass over the silver foil, Leah arbitrarily trails transparent glasses of different colors over it, as she is doing in the first three photos on the right. First she applies amethyst, then light green and finally cobalt. As with casing cane, she picks dark transparent colors for this application because of the rich depth of color that they bring to the bead.

You can see how she is randomly trailing the colors onto the bead, criss-crossing back and forth over the silver foil. With this technique, not only will you have the original colors you applied over the silver, but you will also create a number of new hues from the combinations where the transparent colors overlap. Another way to add the transparent colors would be to dot them onto the silver. This technique could be used to minimize the overlay of one color on another, but it requires much more time than trailing. A combination of these two techniques, referred to as stippling, when you dot rapidly over the surface of the foil taking great care not to burn off any trailing glass threads, can also be an effective means of applying glass randomly over the foil.

After a little while you will have a random coating of transparent glasses as seen in the third photo on this page. At this point, you might want to partially marver out the glass as Leah is doing in the next photo, even if you have not applied all the transparent glass that you want to include, because

it will help prevent trapping any air under the glass. In this case, Leah applies more transparent glass to foil, including the transparent turquoise that we see her adding in the next photo.

Finally, Leah decides that she has added enough transparent glass to the bead and starts to marver it out into a thin uniform coating over the silver. This is what she is doing in the last photo on the previous page; smoothing out the glass by rolling it on her paddle. As she does this, she ensures that some of the transparent glass flows over the edges of the foil onto the base glass of the bead. This will serve to completely anchor the foil to the surface of the bead. This is what she is carefully doing on the first picture on this page.

Finally all of the marvering is finished and the soft pastel Monet background of the bead is complete. The completed background can be seen in the second photo to the left. The transparent overlays give the bead a subtle interplay of color to which this photo does not do justice. The wrinkling of the foil seen in the photo serves as an added decorative feature of the bead background.

Now with the Monet background completed, it is time for Leah to add her floral decorations. In this case, the flowers to be added are violets that grow out of one end of the bead and reach for the sky at the other end. If you remember, Leah makes her violets by first applying three downward strokes of doubly cased cane on the top half of the flower, as she is doing in the third photo on this page, followed by two upward strokes to the center on the bottom half of the flower. The doubly cased cane that she is using is a thin casing of transparent cobalt over opaque white followed with a thick coating of amethyst.

A close up of a finished violet can be seen in the lower left photo. Notice the color variations that result from the casing and how the glass is applied give the flower a very natural appearance. Leah adds four or five of these flowers around the circumference of the bead. They are only placed in what is designated as the upper half of the bead; anywhere from the equator to the top of the bead, as this one is placed. She varies the elevation of the flowers from the equator as she goes around the circumference of the bead to make it look more lifelike.

Next Leah adds the stems of the flowers. These are made using the transparent emerald over white cased cane. She draws these stems starting at

the flower and going down to the bottom of the bead. She goes in this direction because it is easier to control how the stem connects to the flower. If you go the other way, it is hard to burn off the stem right at the flower. See how she curves these stems so that they appear to be bending under the weight of the flower. Notice where she attaches the stem to the flower. She comes in at one of the gaps on either side of the flower. When you apply thin cane like this, you have to work it at the right temperature at the edge of the flame to get it to flow on uniformly.

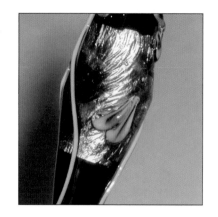

With all the flower stems in place, Lean fills in some of the bare spaces on the bead with leaves. The leaves that she uses on this bead are some of the double wide leaves made from two strokes of the same cased cane as the stems. A close up of one of these leaves can be seen in the photo to the right. See how the two strokes overlap slightly. See how she gets a fair amount of color variation in this leaf. Leah adds about a half dozen of these leaves around the bead.

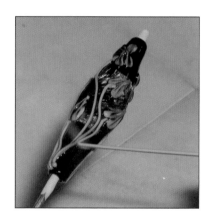

After she has applied all of the leaves that she wants on the bead, she then attaches stems to them. Leah does this as she did for the flowers. She starts the stem at the wide end of the leaf and weaves it down to the bottom of the bead in graceful arcs to give it the feel of supporting the weight of the leaf. If she has the chance, she has it join with one of the flower stems as she trails it down toward the bottom of the bead. This joining gives the collection of decorations more of a unifying plant-like appearance.

The last thing that Leah does to complete the bead is to add two small yellow dots to each flower at the point where the upward strokes join the flower. This can be seen in the third photo to the right. They represent the stamen area of the flower. The final two photos on this page show two views of the finished bead.

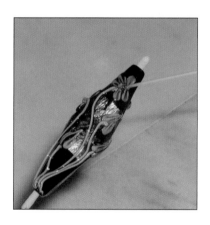

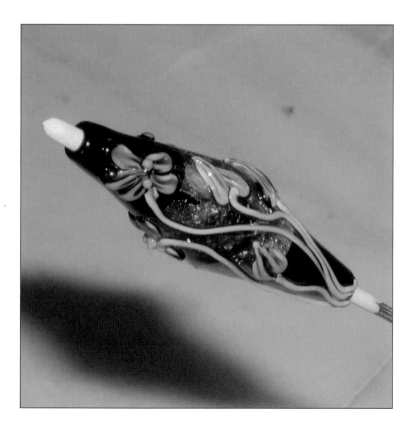

Rainbow Latticino

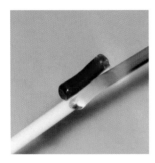

Another kind of construction that Leah makes for use in her work is a fancy form of twisted cane that she calls rainbow latticino. She uses this cane as a lip wrap on some of her beads, such as the urn bead which follows this demonstration.

She starts this construction with an opaque white rod to which she applies axial casings of transparent colors. She adds the axial casing colors as complete sections of transparent rods that she attaches side by side onto the white rod.

She does this by getting about an inch of the opaque rod and one of the transparent rods just hot enough to stick together and lays the transparent rod in place as in the first photo. Then she clips off any extra transparent rod with her tile nippers, as seen in the next photo. You can see how closely these rod sections are laid together in the third photo.

Leah continues to add transparent colors one at a time until they go completely around the white rod. The last transparent rod has to be added just a little hotter to get it to spread out and touch the transparent rods on either side of it. This will make six transparent rods laid up around the white rod as seen in the lower left photo.

To provide better definition to her transition from one color to the next, Leah applies six sections of black filigrana into the valley between each of the six transparent rods, as she is doing in the upper right photo on this page. After all of these are in place the construction will look like the second photo on the right.

Leah then warms up the construction and attaches a stiff transparent handle on the other side. When she does this, she applies a cone of glass on the end of the construction, covering all the rod ends. This cone facilitates uniform pulling over the whole cross section. She then snips off the white core and does the same thing on the other end to make sure it is also well attached. Then she heats the whole thing up and slowly stretches it out while twisting at the same time. You can see how beautiful these turn out in the bottom photo. Unused ends that you may have remain-

ing at the end of the draw can be flattened out and used as earrings or a loop can be added at the end and used as a pendant.

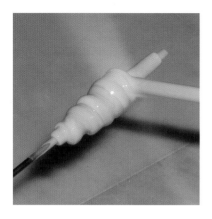 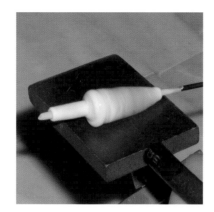 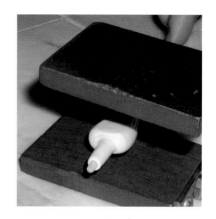

Grape Urn Bead

With this bead, Leah demonstrates making a simple urn shape to which she adds a gold leaf background and grape cluster decorations. The more sculptural shape of this bead contributes an additional level of visual interest over the torpedo shape of the previous beads.

In making the urn shape, Leah starts out as usual by winding glass onto the mandrel in the general shape of the bead. This preform can be seen in the upper left photo. Here she first winds and shapes a small cylindrical bead of the diameter of the vessel's neck. Then, as seen in the photo, she goes back and winds on more glass to form the body of the urn. This tapers from the shoulder of the vessel to its base and resembles half of a torpedo bead. Because of the large difference in the mass between these two areas, the neck cools off much faster than the body of the urn and Leah has to go back frequently and warm it during the construction of this bead.

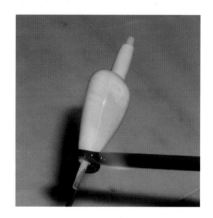

She next shapes the tapered section of the bead on her paddle to smooth it out similar to how she does a torpedo bead. You can see her doing this in the second photo on the top of the page. The area at the shoulder of the vessel is smoothed out on the edge of the paddle. If she wants to smooth out the joint between the cylinder and the body of the vessel, she will roll this area on a small-diameter graphite rod.

Then Leah flattens out the torpedo-shaped section of the bead, to produce her classic 'flattened urn' shape. She does this by heating that portion of the bead and squashing it between two graphite paddles, as seen in the upper right photo. You have to come down straight with the upper paddle as you do this to ensure that the glass is equally displaced on either side of the mandrel. Both sides should be at least the thickness of the mandrel. If either side gets thinner than this, that section may crack later from too rapid cooling. For esthetic reasons she also wants the diameter of the neck to be slightly less than the thickness of the vessel body. An advantage of a flat bead like this is that it will not rotate while it is worn and not as much attention has to be paid to decorating both sides.

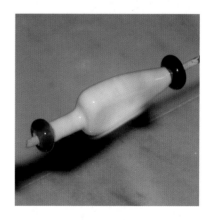

If you look closely at the picture, you will notice that there are some ripples on the flattened surface. These are called chill marks and are caused by the rapid cooling of the bead during shaping with tools. They are removed by reheating the bead in the flame until the marks go away and the surface develops a high gloss as was done prior to the fourth photo.

In the next photo, Leah is adding a wrap of transparent purple to form the lip and foot of the urn. She does this by wrapping a disk of glass at these two locations and then heating the disks up until they collapse into the desired shape. Next, she heats up the body of the bead and covers its surface with gold leaf using her tweezers, as was described earlier. We see her burnishing the gold leaf onto the surface of the bead in the last photo on the previous page.

Now it is time to add handles to the urn. Leah starts by getting the end of a rod of transparent purple slightly molten and attaching it about half-way down the body of the vessel, as seen in the upper left photo. She warms up the bead slightly in the area where the handle will be attached, in order to get the glass to stick. In the following photo, we see her heating up a section of the transparent rod to bend it toward the body of the bead. As she is doing this, she tries to avoid heating the bead too much and burning off some of the gold leaf. This is actually the second bend that she is putting into the handle. The first was at the base of the handle, just above the attachment point.

She continues heating and bending the transparent handle until she gets it attached to the shoulder of the vessel. Then she bends it out slightly and cuts off any excess rod with the flame, as seen in the third photo to the left. She wants to have just a little outward flip of the material remaining at that point.

Next, Leah adds the handle onto the other side of the vessel in the same manner. She then adjusts the final shape of each handle by lightly reheating it and using her tungsten pick to tweak it. She lifts the handle by running her pick along the inside contour to develop a nice pleasing arc to each handle. In the lower left photo, she is using her pick to shape the upper contact area of the handle and ensure that this area is well attached to the vessel.

With handle shaping completed, she next adds a lip wrap of her rainbow latticino to the top of the vessel. Because this cane is fairly small in diameter, she applies it through the side of the flame for better control. She wraps it all the way around the lip and burns off any excess. In the last photo on this page, we see a close up of the finished lip wrap and of the bead background prior to applying any of the grape decorations. Notice that some of the gold leaf has burned off near the base and the neck of the urn. Leah could, if

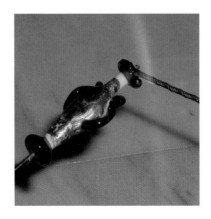

she wanted, go back and recoat these areas, but since much of the surface will be covered by grapes, she decides not to because it also gives the bead a rustic look.

With the background done, Leah now starts work on the grape decorations. In the first photo on this page, she begins by laying out the position of the grape bunches on the urn. She does this by dotting in the outline of each bunch onto the surface of the urn. They are shaped like upside-down raindrops. Notice how she spaces the two bunches so that they cover a large portion of the bead surface but still leave room for tendrils.

Next Leah builds up the bunches grape by grape by successively dotting a doubly cased grape cane, which is made up of a thin casing of transparent cobalt over opaque white followed by a thick casing of transparent amethyst. Because this doubly cased cane is relatively small in diameter, Leah is, as you can see in the first two photos, applying it through the right edge of the torch flame. She is trying to keep the size of these grapes relatively constant as she dots them on.

One of the things that Leah prides herself on is the three dimensionality of her decorations. Therefore, instead of just covering the area of the grape bunch with a single layer of grapes, she builds up the bunches with multiple layers until it develops the material fullness of bunches of natural grape clusters found on the vine. You can see a close up of the two bunches in the third photo on this page.

With the grape bunches in place, Leah now adds the vines and tendrils to the bead. For this purpose, she uses some of her branch cane. First, she adds the vine connections to each of the bunches. These start at the center of the rounded upper end of the bunch and go upward to the neck of the urn. Notice how she applies multiple layers of the branch cane to the thicker sections of the vine.

After completing the vine, she finishes up the decoration by adding tendrils. For these, she lays branch cane onto the surface of the bead, giving it a loose swirled appearance. This is what you see her doing in the second to the last photo. With this, the bead is complete and can be seen in the bottom right photo.

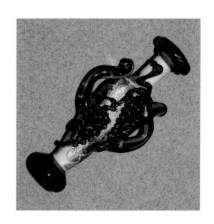

Using Beads in Jewelry

Leah makes a lot of finished jewelry, especially necklaces, from her beads. She does this because there's a market for them. Many patrons do not know what to do with loose beads, they want finished jewelry that they can wear.

Part of the challenge in designing finished jewelry that incorporates your handmade beads, is to keep the jewelry affordable. If you include more than a few handmade beads into a piece, in order for you to make a decent wage cost of the piece would be too high. So the goal is to come up with jewelry designs that make effective use of your handmade beads; for example, use them as focal points in works which are made up largely of more economical commercial beads.

When choosing commercial beads, it is important to consider both their color and quality. Leah tries to select beads that pick up the accent colors of the floral beads that she is going to include in the piece. She will pick out one or two colors from a floral decoration and will purchase commercial beads that are close to those colors. For design purposes, the piece will often be more interesting if the beads are of different sizes. Then

**Goddess Necklace, 1998
Photo by: George Post**

besides color differences between the beads, you will have variations in the size of the beads to tickle the eye.

The simplest design is to place your handmade bead front and center as seen in the photo above. If you want to you could also space a couple of small handmade beads on either side of the centerpiece floral bead. Unless the focal bead is very large or loud, you may want to work on bringing more attention to it. Leah often does this by adding a beaded tassel to the focus bead as seen to the right. The larger mass and the movement of the tassels help draw one's eye to the region.

If she has the right sizes of beads available, Leah likes to graduate the beads as she approaches the larger focus bead. These larger beads may be interspersed with smaller separator beads. They can be added either symmetrically or asymmetrically around the center focus bead. If placed asymmetrically, you have to work at balancing the actual and visual mass of the beads to get them to hang and look right. Leah does this by doing something like balancing three medium-sized handmade beads on one side of the necklace with a large and a small pair on the other side.

**Grape Fountain Necklace, 1998
Photo by: George Post**

Simple Iris Choker, 2001

Another thing that Leah has started doing lately is working on collaborations with other jewelry artists, in particular artists who work in metals. This helps add a new dimension to her work. She has also started collaborating with her husband by leaving a portion of her bead undecorated so that he can cold work part of the bead to give it facets to add to its sparkle.

Again as always, these suggestions are just guides. There are many different ways that these ideas can be put together. Use the pictures of Leah's necklaces included in this booklet as examples to inspire your work.